"A Journey into Poland's Hidden Gem"

Jayden Gray

Szczecin

Travel Guide

2023

Table of Contents

INTRODUCTION: UNVEILING SZCZECIN'S HIDDEN CHARMS

Szczecin, which is tucked away along the banks of the Oder River, is a fascinating but sometimes disregarded jewel in Poland's rich cultural tapestry. Prepare to be mesmerized as you travel around this fascinating city by its historical importance, thriving cultural scene, and a feeling of hidden charm that sets it different from other popular European travel locations.

- **Welcome to Szczecin**

There is a sense of eagerness and intrigue as soon as you arrive in Szczecin. Visitors are greeted warmly by the city, which offers them a special fusion of contemporary attractiveness and ancient mystery. The contrast of architectural forms seen at first glance in Szczecin's skyline reflects the city's extensive history of cultural influences from many eras. Stunning spires, elaborate facades, and modern construction coexist peacefully in this city that has gently changed through time.

The people of the city, who are renowned for their warmth and genuine friendliness, greatly contribute to creating a friendly environment. Locals often strike up talks with tourists, eager to share their pride in Szczecin's history and provide insider tips. This friendliness, together with the city's distinctive personality, creates the ideal environment for an enjoyable exploration.

- **Why Szczecin? Discovering the Hidden Gem**

Szczecin provides a welcome respite for anyone seeking a more genuine and personal travel experience in an age of mass tourism when many popular places often bustle with tourists. But what distinguishes Szczecin as a jewel worth unearthing?

A Rich Historical Narrative

Szczecin, located in the nexus of European history, has a rich past rich in tales of monarchs and conquerors. The city's architecture acts as a direct connection to its history, from medieval walls to the imperial magnificence of Ducal Castle. Every cobblestone road whispers stories of resilience and change, luring you to explore the history of a city that has withstood the passage of time.

Cultural Kaleidoscope

Szczecin flourishes as a center of cultural variety and creative expression in addition to its historical importance. Theaters, galleries, and performance venues in the city are humming with cultural energy and provide a wide range of experiences to suit all tastes. Szczecin's cultural landscape captivates the senses and urges you to engage in its lively creative energy, whether you're attracted to classical symphonies at the

Philharmonic or contemporary exhibits at neighborhood galleries.

Off-the-Beaten-Path Discoveries

The attentive tourist should investigate the inconspicuous areas of Szczecin to discover its charm. The city invites you to roam, rewarding your curiosity with secret courtyards, adorable shops, and unexpected gastronomic pleasures, in contrast to better-traveled roads. You'll find a lovely contrast between old and new as you walk through its streets, providing a real feeling of discovery at every turn.

A Sense of Tranquil Beauty

The Oder River brings a sense of peace to Szczecin's metropolitan environment with its calm waters and scenic promenades. The river's presence provides a calming background that contrasts with the intensity of the city, whether you're taking a leisurely walk along the waterfront or taking a tranquil boat trip. This fusion of urban energy and scenic beauty results in a harmonious environment that is distinctively Szczecin.

We'll dive more into the facets that make up Szczecin's buried charms in the parts that follow. Each aspect of the city enhances its appeal, from its historical landmarks and cultural attractions to its culinary scene and lesser-known activities. So come along with us as we go on a discovery tour of Szczecin, a city that encourages you to find its hidden treasures and make your own unforgettable experiences.

TRACING HISTORY AND CULTURE: UNVEILING SZCZECIN'S RICH HERITAGE

Szczecin, a city rich in culture and history, invites visitors to take a trip through time and creative expression. Szczecin's tapestry of history and culture crafts a tale that captivates the senses and excites the imagination, from its medieval beginnings to its thriving modern art scene. The layers of Szczecin's history are explored in this part, along with the city's past, cultural influences, and vibrant creative scene.

- **A Glimpse into Szczecin's Past**

The architecture, monuments, and timeless tales of Szczecin bring the city's rich past to life as you walk the streets. Szczecin, which dates back to the eighth century, has seen several invasions, rulers, and changes that have permanently altered its character.

Medieval Fortification and Royal Legacy

The vestiges of Szczecin's medieval fortifications, which once served as a key commercial hub and a center of power, provide a window into the city's history. These fortifications include city walls, watchtowers, and gates. As a focal point that has seen centuries of development, the Ducal Castle remains a regal tribute to the city's royal legacy.

World Wars and Rebuilding

Szczecin was left in ruins and had most of its ancient architecture destroyed by the wounds of World War II. However, the city's post-war reconstruction efforts demonstrate its resiliency. Historic buildings like the Philharmonic building and the Pomeranian Dukes' Castle have been given new life via architectural conservation and restoration initiatives, safeguarding their historical relevance for future generations.

Szczecin Museum: Guardians of History

An immersive voyage into history is provided by the Museum of Szczecin, which has many locations spread around the city. Several museums, including the National Museum and the Maritime Museum, include relics, works of art, and exhibitions that tell the history of Szczecin from many perspectives. These organizations provide a comprehensive view of the development of the city, ranging from marine customs to medieval antiquities.

- **Cultural Mosaic: Influences and Traditions**

The cultural fabric of Szczecin is made up of a tapestry of influences that have influenced the city's character throughout time. The city's cultural mosaic is proof of the peaceful coexistence of many cultures and backgrounds since it is located at the intersection of trade routes and is home to varied people.

Hanseatic Legacy

Szczecin's history is entwined with the commerce network that covered the Baltic Sea area since it was a founding member of the Hanseatic League. The architecture, maritime history, and even the gastronomy of the city all have strong Hanseatic influences. Festivals and activities that recognize this historical link continue to commemorate the Hanseatic League's history.

German and Polish Ties

Due to Szczecin's position on the border of Poland and Germany, a fusion of Polish and German influences may be seen in its culture. The city's fluctuating demographics and identities have produced a vibrant cultural fabric that blends German and Polish traditions. This cultural intersection may be seen in the city's architecture, language, and even gastronomic offerings, resulting in a distinctive blend.

Religious Diversity

Szczecin's unique religious environment contributes to the city's cultural diversity. The city's religious structures, which range from ancient churches to synagogues and mosques, serve as reminders of tradition and religion. With its impressive spires, the Church of St. Peter and St. Paul is a well-known monument that personifies Szczecin's spiritual importance.

- **Contemporary Arts and Creative Scene**

Szczecin's cultural journey extends beyond its past; it also serves as a vibrant center for modern art and free expression. Galleries, theaters, and events that feature both local and foreign talent are abundant in the city's creative scene.

Philharmonic of Szczecin: A Melodic Marvel

The Szczecin Philharmonic, a work of architecture in and of itself, provides a symphonic experience that reflects the cultural uniqueness of the city. Its acoustics and architecture have brought it recognition on a global scale, attracting both fans of classical music and novices. You may experience the musical essence of the city by attending a concert here.

Galleries and Arts Spaces

The gallery scene in Szczecin offers a venue for artists to display their creations, from classic paintings to cutting-edge installations. In the old arsenal building's Arsenal Gallery, a variety of artistic mediums are on display. Other art venues and galleries, such as 13 Muz Gallery, also add to the city's creative vitality.

Cultural Festivals and Events

The calendar of Szczecin is filled with festivals and cultural events that honor everything from music and theater to literature and movies. The city's dedication to encouraging creativity and accepting variety is shown by the OFF Cinema Film Festival, Szczecin European Film Festival, and Music on the Odra Festival.

Finally, Szczecin's history and culture provide a rich, multi-layered tapestry that beckons investigation and reflection. The city's history and present are intertwined to create an ambiance that is both beautiful and educational, from its medieval beginnings to its modern creative scene. You'll learn that Szczecin values its past while advancing in the direction of the present as you explore its history, traverse its cultural influences, and immerse yourself in its creative representations.

GETTING TO SZCZECIN: EXPLORING YOUR TRANSPORTATION OPTIONS

The voyage to Szczecin, Poland's undiscovered treasure, is an exhilarating prologue to the adventures that are in store for you there. The variety of travel alternatives makes getting to Szczecin simple and enjoyable, whether you're traveling from a nearby city or a far-off nation. In this part, we'll examine the many approaches to getting to the city, outlining the available forms of transportation and offering advice to make the most of your travel arrangements.

- **Transportation Options**

The first step in discovering Szczecin's attractions is to decide how you'll get there. Due to its advantageous location, the city is easily accessible by a variety of transportation options. There are many different modes of transportation available, from land to sea, so you may choose the one that best matches your interests and manner of travel.

By Car: Navigating the Roadways

Driving to Szczecin provides a feeling of independence and the chance to see Poland's beautiful landscapes for vacationers who value the adaptability of their wheels. A vast network of motorways and well-maintained roadways provide excellent access to the city.

Traveling by car to Szczecin from adjacent cities like Berlin or Gdansk may be an experience in and of itself. Remember that the majority of the road signs are in Polish, so having a map or navigation software ready might assist in guaranteeing a smooth ride.

By Train: Embracing the Railways

Train travel is a great method to go to Szczecin because of how effective and connected the Polish rail network is. Szczecin Główny, the city's principal railway station, is conveniently situated and acts as a significant hub for both domestic and foreign trains.

Arriving from Warsaw, Krakow, or other Polish towns, you may take advantage of a relaxing voyage on contemporary trains that come equipped with features like Wi-Fi and food options. Train links from Berlin and other European cities to Szczecin offer an attractive and hassle-free trip for visitors from outside.

By Bus: Exploring Bus Networks

An affordable and practical method to go to Szczecin is via bus. Numerous domestic and foreign bus companies run routes into the city, giving passengers a variety of alternatives. Buses have variable departure hours and are a good option for anybody looking for a cheap means of transportation. The major bus station in Szczecin receives a large number of buses, providing quick access to the city's attractions and downtown.

- **Arrival by Air, Train, and Bus**

Arriving by Air: Szczecin-Goleniów Airport

Szczecin-Goleniów Airport (SZZ) is the main entry point for visitors coming from far-off places or nearby nations. This contemporary airport provides a handy entrance point for travelers from abroad and is located around 45 kilometers northeast of the city center. With flights run by numerous airlines, the airport is well-connected to major European destinations including London, Dublin, and Oslo.

After touching down at Szczecin-Goleniów Airport, there are many ways to get to the city's core. There are several taxis and ride-sharing services that provide convenient and hassle-free travel. Additionally, public buses provide affordable transportation and run routes from the airport to important locations in Szczecin. Due to the airport's proximity to the city, you can easily go from the runway to the center of Szczecin's secret attractions.

Arriving by Train: Szczecin Główny Station

The Szczecin Główny Station is a notable sight and an important transit hub if you decide to come by rail. You will be in a good position to explore the city once you arrive thanks to the station's convenient location. There are ticket booths, waiting areas, and numerous services available at the station's contemporary amenities to meet your requirements.

You can quickly visit the city's many areas and attractions from Szczecin Główny Station thanks to its effective public transit system. You can easily get about the city via the trams and buses, and using Szczecin's public transportation is both simple and enjoyable.

Arriving by Bus: Main Bus Terminal

You will likely arrive in Szczecin's Main Bus Terminal if you choose to take a bus. This thriving center provides access to several locations throughout Poland and its neighbors. Similar to the railway station, the bus terminal's strategic position puts Szczecin's urban fabric within easy reach.

You may easily change to local buses or trams that crisscross the city and provide you access to its many attractions from the Main Bus Terminal. Exploring Szczecin is efficient and pleasurable because of the seamless integration of various transportation options.

In conclusion, accessibility and ease characterize the trip to Szczecin. The city's transportation choices may accommodate a variety of tastes and travel types whether you are traveling by plane, train, or bus.

As you set out on your expedition, know that getting to Szczecin is not only a means to an end but an essential component of the adventure—a doorway to the hidden beauties that this alluring Polish city has to offer.

ACCOMMODATION: A HOME AWAY FROM HOME IN SZCZECIN

The appropriate lodging sets the tone for your whole trip, and Szczecin has a wide range of alternatives to suit different tastes and budgets. The city makes sure that every guest gets a lodging option that fits their personality, from opulent hotels to endearing bed & breakfasts and cost-effective budget lodgings. In this part, we'll examine Szczecin's lodging options, providing details on the many kinds of accommodations that are available and showcasing some of the best hotels in the area.

- **Hotels and Lodges: Luxury and Comfort**

Szczecin's hotels and lodges provide an elegant hideaway for visitors seeking a sumptuous escape with first-rate service. These lodgings provide a balance of comfort, elegance, and convenience whether you're traveling for a business trip, a romantic break, or just to unwind.

Hotel Aria Boutique
Address: Aleja Wojska Polskiego 75, 70-481 Szczecin.

The luxurious and sophisticated Hotel Aria Boutique is tucked away in the center of the city. Modern conveniences and beautiful décor combine in the opulent rooms and suites to create a quiet atmosphere that envelops you in peace. A great visit is guaranteed with the hotel's excellent dining restaurant, spa amenities, and attentive personnel.

Radisson Blu Szczecin
Address: Plac Rodła 10, 70-419 Szczecin

The Radisson Blu Szczecin provides a seamless fusion of modern style and first-rate services while boasting spectacular city views. With its wellness center, rooftop bar, and large rooms, the hotel is a great option for discriminating guests and offers convenient access to the city's major attractions.

- **Bed and Breakfasts: Charming Retreats**

Szczecin's bed and breakfasts provide a pleasant refuge that seems like a home away from home for tourists who like a more intimate and customized experience. These lovely accommodations provide a chance to interact with regional hosts and other guests, building a feeling of community.

B&B Cozy Corner
Address: ul. Kręta 13a, 71-788 Szczecin

B&B Cozy Corner, tucked away in a peaceful area, extends a kind greeting to all visitors. The shared areas promote connection with other guests, while the attractively decorated apartments radiate a cozy appeal. Your stay will have an extra genuine feel thanks to the excellent prepared breakfast.

Apartamenty B&B Marie

Address: ul. Wiosny Ludów 16/4, 71-514 Szczecin

The well-appointed rooms at Apartamenty B&B Marie combine comfort and flair, and the hosts provide individualized service. It serves as a great home base for visiting the city's attractions thanks to its welcoming décor and handy location. Your trip is made more real by the hosts' suggestions and perceptions of local culture.

- **Budget Accommodations: Affordable Explorations**

Budget travel in Szczecin does not necessitate forgoing comfort or convenience. The city has affordable lodging options that are good value for money, letting you discover its secret attractions without breaking the bank.

Campanile Hotel Szczecin
Address: ul. Wyszyński 30, 70-203 Szczecin.

The accommodations of the Campanile Hotel Szczecin are reasonably priced without sacrificing comfort. The hotel's contemporary style and practical facilities make it a great option for guests on a tight budget. The on-site restaurant offers a wide selection of food to suit diverse palates.

Ibis Budget Szczecin
Address: ul. Dworcowa 16, 70-206 Szczecin.

Ibis Budget Szczecin offers simple yet welcoming lodgings in a convenient location at a low cost. Travelers who prefer to explore the city over opulent facilities will find it to be a sensible option since the rooms are created to maximize space. The hotel's uncomplicated philosophy guarantees a stress-free stay.

- **Top Hotels in Szczecin: Luxury and Distinction**

While Szczecin has a variety of hotels, certain of them stand out for their superior service, features, and atmosphere. The following top hotels personify Szczecin's friendliness and allure:

Radisson Blu Szczecin
Address: Plac Roda 10, 70-419 Szczecin,

The Radisson Blu Szczecin provides a seamless fusion of modern style and first-rate services while boasting spectacular city views. With its wellness center, rooftop bar, and large rooms, the hotel is a great option for discriminating guests and offers convenient access to the city's major attractions.

Park Hotel

Address: ul. Plantowa 1, 70-527 Szczecin

The Park Hotel has a posh, tranquil atmosphere since it is surrounded by beautiful vegetation. The hotel's restaurant and bar provide delectable cuisine and a peaceful atmosphere, while the well-appointed rooms and suites are built for comfort. Within the metropolis, there is calm to be found at the nearby park.

Dana Hotel & Spa
Address: ul. Wyzwolenia 13, 70-571 Szczecin

The Dana Hotel & Spa welcomes visitors to rest in its spa areas and take in a tranquil atmosphere. A refreshing stay is made possible by the contemporary accommodations, wellness features, and on-site food choices. You can easily see the sights in Szczecin because of the hotel's proximity to the city center.

In conclusion, Szczecin's lodging options suit visitors of various tastes and financial abilities.

The city provides a broad range of accommodations, so your stay will be more than simply a place to sleep but an essential component of your discovery of Szczecin's hidden jewels, whether you're looking for luxury, warmth, or affordability. Every form of shelter, from hotels and bed and breakfasts to low-cost lodgings, adds to the city's warm embrace and invites you to experience its beauty and authenticity for yourself.

CULINARY EXPEDITION: TASTING SZCZECIN'S DISTINCTIVE FLAVORS

Through each delicious mouthful, embarking on a culinary tour of Szczecin is like traveling through the city's history, culture, and marine spirit. The culinary scene in Szczecin is a reflection of the city's rich legacy and a monument to the inventiveness of its chefs, and it ranges from traditional Polish dishes to seafood delights that honor the city's seaside position.

The intricacies of Szczecin's culinary scene are explored in this part as we dig into its regional specialties, seafood selections, and lovely waterfront restaurants.

- Savoring Local Flavors

The ability to combine classic Polish cuisine with modern adaptations to produce meals that are both familiar and inventive is at the core of Szczecin's culinary character. You'll experience a symphony of sensations as you explore the city's restaurants, paying respect to its history while embracing contemporary culinary trends.

Pierogi: Polish Dumplings with a Twist

Pierogi are a staple of Polish cuisine, and Szczecin gives its distinctive take on this well-known delicacy. While classic pierogi are a mainstay, many creative versions highlight regional ingredients and international influences.

Pierogi are a monument to the culinary innovation that characterizes Szczecin's eating scene, ranging from savory contents like cabbage and mushrooms to sweet versions packed with berries or sweet cheese.

Bigos: The Hunter's Stew

Bigos, sometimes known as "hunter's stew," is a filling meal that epitomizes Polish comfort cuisine. This stew, which combines sauerkraut, fresh cabbage, and different meats, exhibits the city's love of strong tastes. Each bowl of bigos is a unique gastronomic experience since each chef gives the dish their personal touch.

- **Seafood Delights and Culinary Heritage**

It is not surprising that seafood is a key ingredient in the cuisine of Szczecin given its position along the Oder River and closeness to the Baltic Sea. Dishes that honor both the riches of the sea and the city's culinary legacy have been created as a result of the blending of marine influence and local customs.

Smoked Fish: Maritime Tradition

A distinctive position in Szczecin's culinary legacy belongs to smoked fish. Fish caught in the area is preserved thanks to the city's long-standing custom of smoking it, which also elevates it to a delicious delicacy. To enjoy smoked herring, mackerel, and other species that capture the city's marine spirit, visit nearby markets and smokehouses.

Fish Soup: A Taste of the Baltic

"Zupa rybna," or fish soup, delivers a taste of the riches of the Baltic Sea. This rich soup, made with a combination of fish, vegetables, and flavorful spices, perfectly expresses Szczecin's marine heritage. Fish soup is a gastronomic voyage through the tastes of the sea, whether it is eaten at a neighborhood pub or a restaurant by the ocean.

- **Dining with a View: Waterside Eateries**

You'll discover that Szczecin's waterfront restaurants give more than just sustenance as you indulge in the city's delectable cuisine—they offer a memorable dining experience that embraces the majesty of the Oder River and the city's picturesque scenery.

Restauracja Horyzont

Restauracja Horyzont, perched atop the Radisson Blu Hotel, provides sweeping views of both the city and the Oder River. The restaurant's stunning setting complements its extensive menu, which features Polish and foreign cuisine. This restaurant offers a gastronomic experience that appeals to all the senses whether you dine during the day or at night.

Majestic Pomerania Cruise and Restaurant

Majestic Pomerania provides a unique dining experience by combining a gourmet trip with a river cruise. The restaurant's cuisine places a strong emphasis on fresh seafood in honor of the city's marine history. One of the most intriguing and memorable ways to see Szczecin is to eat while cruising along a boat on the Oder River.

- **Wrapping up the Culinary Expedition**

As your gastronomic tour of Szczecin comes to a close, you'll discover that the city's tastes are just as varied as its history and culture. Every taste conveys a tale that connects with both the past and the present, from traditional Polish cuisine to seafood delicacies that reflect its marine nature.

Every culinary adventure in Szczecin is a voyage of taste and discovery, whether you're enjoying pierogi with a modern twist, enjoying the coziness of bigos, or delighting in smoked salmon by the river. The city's waterfront restaurants provide the ideal setting, enticing you to eat while admiring the Oder River.

This serves as a reminder that Szczecin's culinary pleasures are more than simply food; they are also a way to experience the city's essence, history, and character.

NAVIGATING THE CITYSCAPE: EXPLORING SZCZECIN'S ARCHITECTURAL MARVELS AND HIDDEN GEMS

The cityscape of Szczecin is an amazing fusion of magnificent architectural structures, tranquil urban green areas, and endearing undiscovered nooks. You'll discover a fascinating tapestry of history, invention, and everyday life as you walk through its streets.

This section delves into the many layers of Szczecin's urban landscape, from its majestic monuments to its off-the-beaten-track gems.

- **Architectural Marvels and Historic Landmarks**

The buildings of Szczecin are a living record of the city's past, from the Middle Ages to the present. The spires, facades, and other buildings that line the city's skyline serve as reminders of its historical significance and progression through time.

Ducal Castle: A Regal Legacy

The Ducal Castle is a marvel of architecture and a significant historical site located in the center of Szczecin. The castle, whose beginnings date to the 14th century, has seen the rise and fall of several empires, making it a witness to the city's development. The Gothic and Renaissance features of the castle, as well as its lovely courtyard, entice tourists to learn more about its colorful history.

Pomeranian Dukes' Castle: History Preserved

Another architectural gem in Szczecin is The Pomeranian Dukes' Castle, which exemplifies the city's dedication to historical preservation. The National Museum of Szczecin is currently housed in this opulent building that was originally a royal home. Its painstakingly renovated rooms and exhibits provide a window into the history, culture, and art of the area.

- **Urban Greenery: Parks and Gardens**

Despite being well-known for its historical riches, Szczecin also provides a welcome retreat into nature inside its metropolitan setting. The city is filled with parks and gardens that invite locals and tourists to relax in the peace of verdant green areas.

Żeromski: A Riverside Oasis

Located along the Oder River, Żeromski Park provides a tranquil haven away from the bustle of the city. The park's meandering walks, shady avenues, and stunning river vistas provide a tranquil but energizing atmosphere. You may take a break from the hustle and bustle of the city and reconnect with the beauty of nature by taking a leisurely walk around Żeromski Park.

Rose Garden: Blossoms in Bloom

Within Kasprowicz Park, Szczecin's Rose Garden is a floral oasis that is enchanting with its vivid blossoms and alluring scents. The garden, which is home to more than a thousand different kinds of roses, welcomes you to stroll down its pathways lined with vibrant colors while it provides moments of peace and inspiration despite the bustle of the city.

- **Hidden Corners: Exploring Beyond the Main Streets**

The cityscape of Szczecin is defined by recognizable landmarks, but its main charm comes in the discovery of undiscovered books that showcase its unique local character and personality. A side of the city that begs you to explore, wonder, and choose your route is revealed when you go off the major streets.

Waly Chrobrego Promenade: A Riverside Stroll

The city's ancient promenade, Waly Chrobrego, has a mesmerizing fusion of local life, riverfront vistas, and architecture. The promenade offers a place for strolls, people-watching, and taking in the splendor of the Oder River. It is lined with sculptures, cafés, and seats. This vantage point offers expansive vistas that provide an idyllic and energetic atmosphere.

Kamienica Hetmańska: A Hidden Gem

A historic home in the center of Szczecin called Kamienica Hetmaska exhibits a combination of elegant architecture and endearing features. This hidden treasure perfectly encapsulates the spirit of Szczecin's historic charm with its elaborate exterior and distinguishing features. You are invited to go back in time and see the city's atmosphere from a different angle by exploring the area's cobblestone surrounds and charming passageways.

- **Unveiling the Soul of Szczecin's Cityscape**

Every building in Szczecin's cityscape resonates with history, and every green area provides a haven of peace as you go through the streets. The city's identity—a fusion of its history, present, and future aspirations—is shaped by its architectural wonders, urban greenery, and secret nooks. Every step you take in Szczecin's urban landscape, whether you're admiring royal castles, savoring the peace of parks, or meandering through lovely streets, gets you nearer to the city's core, its residents, and its soul.

GASTRONOMY AND NIGHTLIFE: SAVORING SZCZECIN'S CULINARY TREASURES AND VIBRANT NIGHTS

Szczecin's fascination goes beyond its historical sites and architectural wonders; after hours, it comes to life with a booming food scene and an electrifying nightlife that appeals to all tastes. This section explores the culinary gems, nocturnal moods, and quiet hangouts that draw both residents and tourists to Szczecin, from epicurean delicacies that showcase local cuisines to the entrancing rhythms of the night.

- **Epicurean Adventures: Dining Recommendations**

The gastronomic scene in Szczecin is a reflection of the city's lengthy history, multiculturalism, and marine ties. The city's diners, cafés, and restaurants provide a wide variety of choices that honor both regional Polish cuisine and global influences. Szczecin's gastronomy delivers epicurean excursions that tempt the palate, whether you're looking for a substantial Polish dinner or an avant-garde dining experience.

Stary Browar Kociewski

A refuge for those looking for an authentic Polish dining experience is Stary Browar Kociewski. The restaurant's homey atmosphere and conventional fare honor local culinary traditions. The essence of Polish comfort cuisine is showcased by Stary Browar Kociewski, which features dishes like pierogi, kielbasa, thick stews, and savory soups.

Porto Grande

Porto Grande is a reminder of Szczecin's maritime heritage for those who want a taste of the ocean. The restaurant has varied cuisine with an emphasis on seafood and grilled delicacies that go well with the picturesque views of the Oder River. Porto Grande embodies the spirit of seaside dining, whether you're enjoying freshly caught seafood or sipping maritime-inspired beverages.

- **Sunset to Sunrise: Szczecin's Night Time Vibes**

Szczecin's exciting nightlife emerges when the sun sets, providing a wide range of alternatives for those looking for entertainment, music, and a dynamic environment. The city's nightlife caters to a broad clientele with chic cocktail bars and exciting clubs, making every night out an unforgettable experience.

Metro Music Club

Nightlife icon Metro Music Club has been enthralling people for years. Mctro Music Club is a gathering place for both music enthusiasts and partygoers because of its vibrant environment, live music performances, and range of musical genres. The club's excitement and diverse events guarantee a memorable night out.

Klub Elefunk

Klub Elefunk provides a vibrant, welcoming environment that embraces variety. This club is renowned for its busy dance floor and boisterous clientele, hosting theme parties and DJ performances that cross genres. Klub Elefunk guarantees a fun-filled evening, whether you're a serious dancer or just want to enjoy the music.

- **Café Culture and Cozy Hangouts**

Szczecin's nightlife provides excitement and vitality, yet its café scene and quaint hangouts provide areas for unwinding, introspection, and connection. Szczecin's cafes and hangouts provide welcoming settings that value the practice of slowing down, whether you're looking for a peaceful place to read, participate in conversation, or just enjoy a cup of coffee.

Café 22

With its welcoming atmosphere and plenty of books, Café 22 is a favorite hangout for both coffee drinkers and book lovers. The café's book racks beckon you to rest as the scent of freshly made coffee permeates the space. Café 22 is a peaceful hideaway where you may indulge in a coffee fix or enjoy a delicious delight.

Concept Café

Concept Café is a blend of artistic expression, social interaction, and delicious food. A warm and stimulating atmosphere is created by the café's cutting-edge culinary options and contemporary décor. Concept Café encourages a feeling of connection and creative energy with its delectable food and specialty coffees.

- ## A Feast for the Senses

You'll discover that Szczecin's culinary and nightlife options are as varied as the city's history and culture as you explore them. Szczecin offers a feast for the senses that lasts from dusk to dawn, from indulging in historical Polish delicacies to dancing the night away at exciting clubs.

Szczecin's gastronomic and nocturnal attractions inspire you to make lifelong memories and discover the city's character in a new way, whether you're indulging in culinary treasures, soaking up the city's nightlife, or seeking refuge in small cafés.

RETAIL THERAPY: EXPLORING SZCZECIN'S SHOPPING TREASURES

Shopping in Szczecin is a fun experience that reveals a world of regional specialties, boutique treasures, and one-of-a-kind mementos that embody the city. This section looks into Szczecin's retail environment, bringing you through market wanderings, boutique discoveries, and items to enjoy long after your stay, from lively marketplaces to lovely shops.

- **Market Wanderings: Local Crafts and Produce**

The markets in Szczecin are bustling centers of activity that provide a window into local life as well as a treasure trove of handcrafted goods, seasonal food, and culinary treats. Discovering these markets immerses you in the local culture and gives you a chance to buy locally-made goods.

Plac Żołnierza Polskiego Market

Plac Żołnierza Polskiego Market is a center for regional culture and life. Fresh fruit, regional delicacies, and traditional Polish goods may all be found in plenty at the market. This market is a culinary lover's heaven, with everything from fresh fruits and vegetables to locally produced cheeses and cured meats.

Hala Targowa Market

The Hala Targowa Market, which is situated in the center of Szczecin, is a veritable gold mine of handcrafted goods and delectable foods. The market has a wide variety of vendors offering anything from handcrafted jewelry and apparel to one-of-a-kind home furnishings. You may interact with local craftspeople while exploring Hala Targowa and take home one-of-a-kind items.

- **Boutique Finds: Unique Shopping Experiences**

In addition to the markets, Szczecin's boutique scene provides a carefully chosen collection of one-of-a-kind items that suit a variety of preferences. Boutique shopping in Szczecin is an opportunity to find undiscovered treasures and support regional companies, from clothing to home décor.

Fabryka Rękodzieła Boutique

The Fabryka Rękodzieła Boutique is a refuge for artisanal products and handcrafted items. The store has a wide selection of goods made by regional designers, including jewelry, clothing, pottery, and more. You may interact with the ingenuity and craftsmanship that characterize Szczecin's local scene while shopping here.

Mesklino Concept Store

An epicenter for fashion, lifestyle, and design is Mesklino Concept Store. The shop offers a carefully chosen assortment of apparel, accessories, and home goods that embrace regional and international inspirations while reflecting modern trends. Shopping in Mesklino provides a distinctive experience that honors fashion and originality.

- **Souvenirs to Cherish: Bringing Szczecin Home**

More than just simple keepsakes, souvenirs hold memories and tales from your trip. You may take a bit of Szczecin's charm and personality with you by purchasing one of the many souvenirs the city has to offer.

Amber Jewelry: Baltic Elegance

Szczecin is an excellent spot to get beautiful amber jewelry since amber has a unique role in

Baltic culture. Amber jewelry, whether it be a delicate necklace, a statement ring, or gorgeous earrings, is not only exquisite but also a representation of the area's natural history.

Pomeranian Pottery and Crafts

Discover regional ceramics and crafts that capture the essence of Szczecin. Handmade pottery, textiles, and decorative objects embody the aesthetic spirit of the city and make for thoughtful keepsakes that highlight the talent of regional craftspeople.

- **Shopping as an Exploration**

Each market, boutique, and souvenir store you discover as you browse Szczecin's shopping options gives a distinctive insight into the culture and creativity of the city. Shopping in Szczecin turns into an adventure of discovery and connection, whether you're rummaging through crowded markets, discovering boutique bargains, or choosing trinkets that appeal to your heart. The souvenirs you take back with you not only act as a memento of your stay, but they also include the anecdotes and adventures that will make your time in Szczecin memorable.

NATURE ESCAPES AND OUTDOOR PURSUITS: EMBRACING SZCZECIN'S NATURAL BEAUTY

Beyond its metropolitan setting, Szczecin beckons travelers to submerge themselves in the embrace of nature. This section highlights Szczecin's natural beauty and welcomes you to enjoy the city's outdoor riches, which range from nautical activities that celebrate its waterfront charm to serene parks and exhilarating outdoor pastimes.

- **Waterfront Magic: Maritime Activities**

Szczecin invites you to explore its waterways, take in breathtaking vistas, and partake in nautical adventures with a range of marine activities thanks to its position along the Oder River and proximity to the Baltic Sea.

Kayaking and Canoeing on the Oder River

On the Oder River, kayaking and canoeing provide a distinctive viewpoint of the cityscape of Szczecin. Follow the river's calm currents as you paddle past historical sites and verdant vegetation. Kayaking and canoeing provide a tranquil way to interact with nature and the city's marine spirit, whether you are an expert paddler or a beginner.

Yachting and Sailing Adventures

Szczecin's sailing and yachting options provide an amazing experience for those seeking the rush of the open sea. The waters of the Baltic Sea may be explored by hiring a sailboat or yacht. Sailing is a beloved adventure in Szczecin because of the sea wind, the sound of the waves, and the sense of freedom.

- **Parks and Trails: Nature's Retreats**

Parks and trails located inside the municipal limits provide a peaceful retreat from the bustle of the city. These lush havens provide a safe hideaway for unwinding, having picnics, and appreciating the beauty of nature.

Kasprowicz Park: Serenity in the City

Kasprowicz Park is a calm refuge that enchants its verdant surroundings and serene atmosphere. The park's meandering walks, shady nooks, and peaceful ponds make it an ideal environment for picnics and strolls. Kasprowicz Park provides a verdant haven whether you're looking for some alone time or a fun family adventure.

Szczecin Lagoon Trail: Coastal Splendor

Both bikers and walkers may enjoy a gorgeous experience on the Szczecin Lagoon Trail. This walk, which follows the shore, offers breathtaking views of the lagoon, the sea, and the surroundings. The Szczecin Lagoon Trail immerses you in the natural splendor that characterizes the area, whether you want to explore on foot or two wheels.

- ### Active Szczecin: Cycling and More

Szczecin has a wide range of outdoor sports and adventurous pastimes that inspire you to move your way across the city and its environs.

Cycling Expeditions: Countryside and City

Szczecin residents often use bicycles to see the city's many neighborhoods and scenic surroundings. Cycling provides a hands-on method to see Szczecin's numerous sides, from city trails that pass through historical sites to rural routes that highlight the area's natural beauty.

Golfing Delights: Tee Time Amidst Greenery

The golf courses in Szczecin are a golfer's paradise. Numerous golf clubs in the city have well-designed courses nestled among luxuriant vegetation. Golf is a sport that mixes leisure and relaxation. Tee off with peaceful scenery as your background.

- **Embracing Natures Invitations**

Szczecin's scenic surroundings and outdoor activities invite exploration, relaxation, and connection with the natural components that give the area its unique character. The city's outdoor gems provide a variety of activities that appeal to every interest and degree of activity, whether you're kayaking down the Oder River, trekking through picturesque trails, or setting off on a bike journey.

You'll discover that Szczecin's outdoor activities not only revitalize the body but also nurture the soul, leaving you with priceless memories of your interactions with nature's splendor when you accept nature's invites.

CULTURAL ODYSSEY: EXPLORING MUSEUMS, ARTS AND EVENTS

The cultural landscape of Szczecin is a tapestry made of venues that reveal history, inspire innovation, and highlight the essence of the city. This area encourages you to go around Szczecin on a cultural voyage, with everything from enthralling museum exhibits to theatrical performances that transport you to various realms.

- **Museums Unveiled: Art, History, and Science**

The museums in Szczecin provide insights into the history, arts, and scientific advancements of the city and serve as portals to its past, present, and future. Every museum offers a different viewpoint on the city's character and adds to the city's diverse cultural scene.

National Museum in Szczecin

Szczecin's National Museum is a veritable gold mine of art, history, and culture. The museum, which has numerous locations across the city, presents a variety of exhibits that highlight everything from local history and marine heritage to modern art and archaeological findings. An immersive journey through the facets of Szczecin's identity is offered by the National Museum.

Maritime Museum in Szczecin

Szczecin's Marine Museum provides an engrossing investigation of nautical history and marine customs as a city with strong maritime ties. The museum's displays explore shipbuilding, maritime history, and the city's connection to the water. The Maritime Museum offers an intriguing look into how the water shaped Szczecin's character via antique boats and interactive exhibits.

- **Theatrical Soirees: Performances and Shows**

The cultural environment in Szczecin is not complete without theatrical performances and productions, which immerse viewers in enthralling realms of drama, music, and creative expression. Szczecin's theaters and venues provide a range of possibilities that appeal to various preferences, whether you're a lover of traditional theater or modern acts.

The Szczecin Philharmonic

The Szczecin Philharmonic is a center for the performing arts and classical music. The location holds cultural events that highlight both domestic and foreign talent, including chamber music concerts and symphonic performances. A trip through the world of classical music is promised by attending a performance at the Szczecin Philharmonic in a venue that emanates elegance and acoustical quality.

The Drama Theater in Szczecin

The Drama Theater in Szczecin offers a wide variety of theatrical performances, from traditional plays to modern plays. The theater offers a window into the world of drama and storytelling via its performances, which are distinguished by creative brilliance and thought-provoking storylines. The Drama Theater provides a variety of theatrical soirees, whether you're looking for comedy, meditation, or inspiration.

- **Festival Calendar: Celebrating Szczecin's Spirit**

The city of Szczecin's vibrant energy and dedication to honoring culture, creativity, and community are reflected in its festival calendar. The city's streets are alive with music, art, and colorful energy throughout the year thanks to a multitude of festivals and events.

OFF Cinema Film Festival
Date: Annually in April.

The OFF Cinema Film Festival showcases cutting-edge and provocative movies from all around the globe as it honors independent and alternative cinema. The festival's varied lineup comprises narrative features, documentary films, and short films that defy expectations and push the limits of creativity.

Szczecin European Film Festival
Date: Annually in November

The Szczecin European Film Festival pays respect to European cinema by showcasing a variety of movies that reflect the region's rich cultural diversity. The screenings, panel discussions, and workshops during the festival provide a forum for filmmakers and movie fans to have in-depth debates about the arts, cinema, and the human condition.

A Cultural Voyage

You'll discover that Szczecin's museums, creative events, and festivals provide a voyage that transcends time and place as you set off on a cultural expedition around the city. The cultural scene in Szczecin gives you the chance to engage with the heart and people of the city via historical exploration, dramatic storytelling, and festival celebrations of creativity. Every cultural encounter in Szczecin transforms into a journey that enlightens the intellect and stirs the soul, whether you're admiring works of art in galleries, cheering on actors on stage, or taking part in celebrations.

VENTURING BEYOND: DAYS TRIP FROM SZCZECIN TO EXPLORE SURROUNDING GEMS

While Szczecin is a veritable treasure trove of history, culture, and natural beauty, its environs are just as alluring, providing a variety of day trip alternatives that let you visit nearby cities, islands, and coastal scenery. This section explores the variety of day excursions that may be taken from Szczecin, each of which offers a distinctive experience that reveals the area's diversity.

- **Stargard Szczeciński: A Historical Expedition**

The historical and aesthetically pleasing town of Stargard Szczeciński is located not far from Szczecin. A day excursion to Stargard transports you back in time, providing a look at thriving marketplaces, fortifications from the Middle Ages, and a rich cultural legacy.

St. Mary's Church: Gothic Grandeur

Stargard's skyline is dominated by St. Mary's Church, a magnificent example of Gothic design. The church's striking exterior, minute workmanship, and tall spires are evidence of the town's historical importance. You may get sweeping views of Stargard and its charming environs by exploring the church's interior and ascending the tower.

Stargard Town Hall: A Symbol of Civic Pride.

A spectacular example of Renaissance architecture that captures the affluence and civic pride of the town is the Stargard Town Hall. The elaborate façade, ornamental details, and clock tower of the building provide an atmosphere that takes you back in time. A visit to the Town Hall Square gives a window into everyday life and a chance to experience the distinct mood of the community.

- **Międzyzdroje and Wolin Island: Coastal Charisma**

A day excursion to Międzyzdroje and Wolin Island is the ideal option for a seaside getaway that is rich in natural beauty and marine attractiveness. These locations have a mix of sandy beaches, breathtaking cliffs, and alluring scenery.

Międzyzdroje Pier: A Seaside Promenade

Long, sandy beaches and a lovely pier that extends into the Baltic Sea are two of Międzyzdroje's most notable features. The pier provides expansive views of the coastline and invites you to take strolls, soak in the sea air, and photograph the mesmerizing sunsets. A tranquil environment for leisure is created by the beachfront landscape, which is filled with cafés and stores.

Wolin National Park: Nature's Sanctuary

Wolin National Park, a natural haven that welcomes exploration and adventure, is located on Wolin Island. Dense woods, meadows, and the stunning chalk cliffs of the coastline are just a few of the park's many features. Wolin National Park is a paradise for outdoor lovers looking to connect with the area's unspoiled beauty thanks to its hiking routes, vistas, and possibilities for birding.

- **Uznam and Świnoujście: Island Escapade**

The lovely village of Swinoujscie is located on Uznam Island, which combines maritime history, sandy beaches, and coastal beauty. You may experience history, tranquility, and seaside charm on a day excursion to Uznam.

Świnoujście Lighthouse: Coastal Beacon

A commanding structure that serves as a representation of nautical history and navigation is the Świnoujście Lighthouse. A panorama of the town, the nearby islands, and the vastness of the Baltic Sea may be seen by climbing the lighthouse. The lighthouse provides information on the previous life of lighthouse keepers as well as a reminder of the area's marine ties.

Beaches & Promenade: Seaside Serenity

The promenade and beaches in Świnoujście provide a charming environment for strolls and relaxation. A welcoming environment for sunbathing, beach activities, and waterfront strolls is created by the town's sandy shoreline and lovely coastal buildings. The town's coastline atmosphere and beachfront cafés provide the ideal setting for taking in the Baltic atmosphere.

- **Day Trip Discoveries**

By going outside of Szczecin, you may explore the area's undiscovered attractions and varied landscapes. The day tours from Szczecin provide a variety of experiences that showcase the region's cultural legacy, natural beauty, and marine character, from historical adventures to coastline charisma and island exploits.

Every day excursion turns into a special journey that enhances your discovery of Szczecin, providing fresh viewpoints, rewarding interactions, and memories that deepen your knowledge of the area's charm.

PRACTICAL INSIGHTS FOR A SEAMLESS STAY IN SZCZECIN

Practical factors are very important to take into account as you prepare for your trip to Szczecin to ensure a hassle-free and pleasurable vacation. This section offers helpful advice to make your stay in Szczecin as easy as possible, guiding you through everything from weather concerns to cultural etiquette.

- **Best Times to Visit and Weather Considerations**

The right time of year to visit Szczecin may make all the difference to your enjoyment of the city's outdoor attractions, cultural activities, and food. Your visit might be improved by being aware of the weather and the ideal times to go.

Spring (April to June): Blooming Beauty

Szczecin has warm weather and burgeoning parks and gardens in the spring. It's the perfect season for strolls, outdoor activities, and seeing cultural sights since the city is alive with brilliant flowers. The springtime offers the ability to fully experience regional festivities since it also happens to coincide with festivals and events.

Summer (June to August): Warmth and Festivity

Szczecin has its busiest travel season in the summer when the weather is nice and the days are longer. Parks, waterfront areas, and outdoor cafés in the city are bustling with activity, creating a welcoming environment for sightseeing and mingling. During this season, there are a ton of festivals, concerts, and outdoor activities that let you take in Szczecin's vibrant culture.

Autumn (September to November): Colors and Comfort

Landscapes in Szczecin undergo a vibrant transition in the autumn. The city's parks and natural areas provide a magnificent background for strolls and outdoor activities when the leaves change and the weather cools. Harvest festivals and other cultural events take place throughout the autumn, giving you a chance to learn about local customs.

Winter (December to February): Cozy and Charm

Szczecin's winters are cozy and charming merry. Despite sometimes being frigid, the city's cafés, museums, and interior attractions provide a cozy haven. Holiday markets, performances, and activities that embody the spirit of the season make it the perfect time to enjoy Szczecin's cultural treasures.

- Navigating Language and Local Etiquette

Your interactions and experiences in Szczccin may be substantially improved by being aware of the regional language and customs. Even though most residents speak English, learning a few words in Polish might help you interact with people.

Language Tips

Being able to communicate with people and get through everyday situations may be facilitated by learning a few fundamental Polish words. Your encounters may be improved by using simple greetings, requests for things like food or directions, and thank-yous.

Local Etiquette

- **Greetings:** When welcoming someone, it's customary to give them a strong handshake and make direct eye contact.

Use "Pan" (Mr.) or "Pani" (Mrs.) after addressing persons by their last names and titles.

- **Gift Giving:** Bringing a little gift, such as flowers, chocolates, or wine, is welcomed if you are asked to a local's house. Gifts are often unwrapped right away.

- **Table Manners:** Do not start eating until the host has begun the meal. As an expression of gratitude for the dinner, it's customary to consume everything on your plate.

- **Tipping:** Tipping is expected at cafés and restaurants. It's customary to tip between 10% and 15% for quality service.

- **Essential Travel Tips and Information**

Practical knowledge is necessary to learn about a new city. This vital travel advice will enable you to enjoy your time in Szczecin and guarantee a hassle-free trip.

Payments and Currency

The Polish zloty (PLN) is used as money in Poland. Although most shops take credit and debit cards, it's a good idea to have extra cash on hand for smaller transactions or locations that may not accept cards.

Public Transportation

Trams and buses are part of the effective public transit network in Szczecin. Tickets may be bought from the driver, at kiosks, or ticket machines. When boarding, make sure you authenticate your ticket.

Safety and Health

Travelers may typically feel secure in Szczecin. As with any place you visit, be aware of your surroundings and personal property, particularly in busy places. There are medical services nearby, but it's best to have travel insurance to cover any unforeseen medical costs.

Electricity

Poland uses 230V as its standard voltage and 50Hz as its standard frequency. The sockets have two circular pins and are of the European kind.

Local Food Cuisine

Polish food is robust and savory, and it often includes items like pierogi, bigos, and kielbasa (sausage). Don't pass up the chance to enjoy regional cuisine at restaurants and cafés.

Connectivity

The majority of hotels, cafés, and public spaces have free Wi-Fi. If you need constant access to the internet while you are there, you can also think about buying a local SIM card.

- **Your Journey Waits**

With your practical knowledge in hand, you're prepared to travel across Szczecin smoothly and with enjoyment. You'll be able to completely immerse yourself in the city's cultural riches, outdoor activities, and warm hospitality by taking into account the ideal times to visit, adopting local language and customs, and adhering to crucial travel advice.

Your time in Szczecin is sure to be one to remember, leaving you with priceless memories and a better grasp of this alluring city.

SAFETY, HEALTH AND WELL-BEING: NAVIGATING YOUR JOURNEY IN SZCZECIN

When visiting a new place, it is crucial to ensure your health, safety, and well-being. This section offers in-depth guidance on how to travel in Szczecin with confidence. It discusses emergency contacts, being safe, and preserving your health while you're there.

- **Emergency Contacts and Medical Services**

It's crucial to be ready for any unforeseen circumstances while traveling. To make sure you have the support you need should the need arise, familiarize yourself with the emergency numbers and medical services that are offered.

Emergency Contacts

Medical Emergency: 112
Police: 997
Fire Department: 998

Medical Services

Szczecin features several hospitals, clinics, and medical institutions that provide top-notch medical treatment if you ever need it. Several renowned hospitals are:

- Szczecin Hospital and Pomeranian Medical University
- Szczecin's Independent Public Hospital No. 1
- Clinical Hospital in Szczecin

Pharmacies

Apothecaries, or apteki, are widely dispersed around the city. To locate pharmacies, look for the green cross icon. While most pharmacies are open during normal work hours, some may provide 24-hour service sometimes

- **Staying Safe in Szczecin**

Although Szczecin is usually seen to be secure for tourists, it is advisable to take security measures to protect yourself and have peace of mind while there.

Personal Belongings

Keep your possessions safe, and pay attention to your surroundings, particularly in busy places. Carry assets in a money belt or covert bag; don't flaunt pricey accessories like jewelry or electronics.

Use Public Transportation

Trams, buses, and trains in Szczecin are typically safe to use, but you should still be careful with your possessions. In busy situations, keep your luggage near and be on the lookout for pickpockets.

Night Safety

Szczecin is generally safe at night, however, it's advised to stay in busy, well-lit areas. When touring the city at night, think about going in groups or using a safe mode of transportation.

- **Travel Wellness: Staying Healthy on the Road**

To fully enjoy your trip, it's important to keep your health and well-being while you're on the road. Using these suggestions, you may maintain good health during your visit to Szczecin.

Nutrition and Hydration

Drink lots of water throughout the day to stay hydrated, particularly if you're wandering in the sun or doing vigorous activity. Try some of the local food, which often features flavorful dishes and fresh ingredients.

Sun Protection

Wear sunscreen, a hat, and sunglasses to shield yourself from the sun's rays while visiting outdoor sites. This is crucial in the summertime when the sun may be quite powerful.

Physical Activity

The parks, paths, and outdoor spaces in Szczecin provide chances for exercise. Getting exercise, whether it's a gentle walk or a strenuous trek, may improve your well-being in general.

Rest and Sleep

For you to enjoy your vacation, make sure you get enough sleep. Make sure you receive enough sleep every night so you can start your adventures feeling rested and invigorated.

Local Medical Care

Make sure you pack enough medicine for your trip if you have any current medical issues or need it. In case you need help, do some advanced research on the nearby medical facilities.

- **Your Well-being Matters**

Prioritizing your safety, health, and well-being while you travel around Szczecin will improve your trip. You may completely immerse yourself in the city's cultural pleasures, outdoor pastimes, and local experiences by being ready with emergency contacts, being aware of your surroundings, and keeping your health routines. You can expect your trip to Szczecin to be not only educational but also secure and well-rounded, leaving you with priceless memories of travel and adventure.

POLISH PHRASES FOR CONNECTION: BRIDGING CULTURES IN SZCZECIN

Language is an effective tool for bridging cultural gaps, fostering relationships, and improving travel experiences. You will learn key Polish expressions in this part that will enable you to interact with people, converse, and fully experience Szczecin's rich cultural diversity.

- **Basic Polish Expressions for Travelers**

Understanding a few fundamental Polish terms may improve your communication and show that you appreciate the community. Even though English is widely spoken in Szczecin, making an effort to learn a little Polish will help you connect with more people.

Greetings and Basic Phrases

Hello: Cześć (cheshch)

Good morning: Dzień dobry (dzyen dobri)

Good evening: Dobry wieczór (dobri vyechoor)

Goodbye: Do widzenia (do veedzenya)

Please: Proszę (prosheh)

Thank you: Dziękuję (dzyenkoo-yeh)

Yes: Tak (tahk)

No: Nie (nyeh)

Excuse me / I'm sorry: Przepraszam
(psheh-prasham)

How are you?: Jak się masz? (yahk syeh
mahsh?)

I don't understand: Nie rozumiem (nyeh
rozoo-myeem)

Getting Around

Where is...?: Gdzie jest...? (gdzhyeh yest...)

How much is this?: Ile to kosztuje? (ee-leh toh kohs-too-yeh?)

Ordering Food

I would like...: Poproszę... (poprosheh...)

Water: Woda (voda)

Beer: Piwo (pee-voh)

Coffee: Kawa (kah-vah)

Directions

Left: Lewo (leh-vo)

Right: Prawo (prah-vo)

Straight ahead: Prosto (proh-stoh)

Where is the bathroom?: Gdzie jest toaleta? (gdzhyeh yest toa-letah?)

- **Cultural Insights through Language**

Understanding another culture is facilitated by language. Speaking a few phrases in the native tongue demonstrates your respect for the community and helps you establish a stronger connection with them.

Polish Politeness

Politeness is highly valued in Polish culture. Greetings, "please," and "thank you" should always be used in conversations. In addition, using the proper pronouns (Pan for Mr. and Pani for Mrs.) gives a touch of respect and formality.

Etiquette in Conversation

Before getting into the primary subject of discussion, Polish talks often begin with polite pleasantries and inquiries about well-being.

Before getting to the subject, please take the time to participate in civil dialogue.

Local flavor

Polish speakers are likely to respond with warmth and advice when you order meals or inquire about regional delicacies. Your culinary experiences may be improved and you can feel more connected to the culture by speaking the local language at restaurants and marketplaces.

Breaking the Ice

When speaking with locals, using simple Polish words might be a great icebreaker. Attempting to speak in Polish, even if your pronunciation isn't great, may result in pleasant interactions and unforgettable meetings.

- **Language as a Key to Connection**

You may enter Szczecin and make deep relationships while learning a few basic Polish languages. The manners, phrases, and context of ordinary life are revealed through the local language. Your attempts to communicate in Polish will be recognized and reciprocated, enabling you to create relationships that go beyond words, whether you're ordering food, getting directions, or just having a discussion.

FAREWELL TO SZCZECIN: REFLECTING ON YOUR JOURNEY

Think back on the memorable moments, enlightening encounters, and cultural learnings you've had as your time in Szczecin comes to an end. This section offers suggestions for an easy departure while also encouraging you to say goodbye to Szczecin with appreciation and a feeling of accomplishment.

- **Reflecting on Your Journey**

Consider the events that will live in your memory as you get ready to depart Szczecin. Each encounter has added to your adventure, whether it was discovering the city's historical landmarks, indulging in its gastronomic choices, making friends with locals, or immersing yourself in its cultural attractions. If you want to capture the spirit of your vacation, think about writing down your best experiences, interactions, and thoughts in a travel notebook.

- **Culmination of Cultural Encounters**

Through language, shared meals, or interesting discussions, the contacts you've developed throughout your stay in Szczecin have opened a window into the lively local culture. Take these conversations with you as mementos of your adventure as you say goodbye. Even when you go further, the understanding of regional customs, traditions, and ways of life you've obtained will keep you connected to Szczecin's soul.

- **Embracing Gratitude**

Accept a feeling of thankfulness for the experiences that have enhanced your trip as you bid farewell to Szczecin. Your recollections are woven together by a variety of factors, including the charmingness of the city's parks, the friendliness of its residents, and the tranquility of its shoreline. Spend a time expressing your gratitude for the wonder, introspection, and joy that have infused your days.

- **Practical Departure Insights**

Practical things need to be taken into account as you get ready to leave Szczecin to guarantee a seamless transition.

- **Packaging and Souvenirs**

Think back on the keepsakes and souvenirs you have gathered while you pack your baggage. These trinkets capture the spirit of Szczecin and may act as a travel memento. If you want to be transported back to the magical ambiance of the city, think about leaving room in your suitcase for these gems.

- **Check-out and Travel Documents**

Make sure you check out of any lodgings you are staying in and pay any outstanding debts. To minimize last-minute stress at the airport or train station, arrange your travel paperwork, including passports, tickets, and any required visas.

- **Saying Goodbye**

Saying farewell might be difficult if you've gotten to know locals or other visitors over your stay. If you want to keep in touch and maintain the contacts you've created, provide your contact information. Think about leaving a sincere message or a gift to show your gratitude for the hospitality you've experienced.

- **The Legacy of your Journey**

Remember that your adventure doesn't finish when you leave Szczecin when you say goodbye. Your life will continue to be enriched by the events, realizations, and memories you've gathered. Carry Szczecin's hidden treasures, cultural tapestry, and the friendliness of its residents with you as you go on, knowing that the spirit of the city will continue to be a part of your tale.

- **A Heartfelt Goodbye**

Take a minute to take in the sights, sounds, and feelings of Szczecin one final time before you depart. Each moment has weaved a special tapestry that is yours to keep, whether it is the sweeping views from its architectural wonders, the conversations had over meals, or the bonds created with its citizens. Say goodbye to Szczecin with appreciation for the adventure you've made, knowing that the city's undiscovered beauties and cultural gems will always have a particular place in your heart.

Printed in Great Britain
by Amazon